Sahil A Gosalia

NEW AGE NECESSITIES

Copyright 2023 by Sahil A Gosalia

All rights reserved. No part of this book may be reproduced, stored in a retrieval system, or transmitted in any form or by any means – electronic, mechanical, photocopying, recording, or otherwise – without prior written permission of the copyright owner, except for brief quotations used in reviews or scholarly analysis.

While every effort has been made to ensure the accuracy of the information contained in this book, the author and publisher assume no responsibility for errors or omissions, or for damages resulting from the use of the information contained herein.

This book is intended for informational purposes only and should not be construed as professional advice. Readers should consult with a qualified professional in the relevant field before taking any actions based on the information contained in this book.

Cover design by Sahil A Gosalia

Published by: Independently Published

Disclaimer

The information contained in this book is for general informational purposes only. While the author and publisher have made every effort to ensure that the information is accurate and up-to-date, they make no representations or warranties of any kind, express or implied, about the completeness, accuracy, reliability, suitability, or availability with respect to the book or the information, products, services, or related graphics contained in the book for any purpose.

Any reliance you place on such information is therefore strictly at your own risk. In no event will the author or publisher be liable for any loss or damage including without limitation, indirect or consequential loss or damage, or any loss or damage whatsoever arising from loss of data or profits arising out of, or in connection with, the use of this book.

The inclusion of any company or product in this book does not imply endorsement by the author or publisher. The views expressed in this book are those of the author and do not necessarily reflect the views of any companies or organizations mentioned.

This book is not intended to be a substitute for professional advice or guidance. Readers should consult with a qualified professional in the relevant field before taking any actions based on the information contained in this book.

Preface

In a rapidly changing world, it's easy to overlook the impact of the businesses and industries that shape our daily lives. These companies have become an integral part of modern society, from the smartphones we carry in our pockets to the transportation services we rely on.

"New Age Necessities" is a book that delves into the history, products, and impact of some of the most influential companies in the world. Through a series of in-depth analyses, the book offers insights into the ways in which these companies have transformed our world and become necessities of modern life.

While the companies covered in this book vary in their industries and products, they share a common thread: they have all leveraged technology to disrupt traditional business models and offer new and innovative solutions to age-old problems.

But with this innovation comes a responsibility to consider the potential impact on society and the world at large. "New Age Necessities" encourages readers to think critically about the role of technology and business in our lives, and to consider the ways in which these companies can continue to innovate while also addressing potential drawbacks.

Ultimately, this book serves as a starting point for understanding the complex relationships between technology, business, and society. I hope readers will be inspired to continue exploring these topics and engage in thoughtful conversations about the future of our world.

Dedicated to

This book is dedicated to all the innovators and entrepreneurs who have disrupted industries, created new markets, and shaped the modern world. It is also dedicated to the millions of people who work for the companies featured in this book, from the engineers and designers to the customer service representatives and factory workers. Without their hard work and dedication, these companies would not be the indispensable parts of our lives that they are today. Finally, this book is dedicated to readers who are curious about the stories and impact of the companies that have become New Age Necessities, and who want to learn more about the changing landscape of business and technology.

Introduction

Welcome to **"New Age Necessities,"** a book that explores the world's most influential and innovative companies that have become integral to our daily lives. From the moment we wake up in the morning to the time we go to bed at night, these companies are a constant presence, helping us to navigate our personal and professional lives in ways we could never have imagined just a few decades ago.

In this book, we will take a deep dive into the stories of the companies that have disrupted industries, changed the game, and shaped modern society as we know it. We will explore how they have become essential to our daily routines, and examine the impact they have had on the world.

We will start by examining the tech giants that have transformed the way we search for information, communicate with each other, and do business. From Google, which has revolutionized the way we access and consume information, to

Apple, which has made technology more accessible and intuitive for people around the world, to Microsoft, which has been at the forefront of computer innovation for decades, these companies have changed the way we live, work, and play.

Next, we will look at the e-commerce powerhouses that have made shopping more convenient and accessible than ever before. Amazon, which started as an online bookstore and has now become a one-stop-shop for all our needs, has redefined the way we shop, while Visa and Mastercard have made it easier to make purchases from anywhere in the world.

We will also delve into the world of healthcare and consumer goods, examining the companies that have become synonymous with the products and services we use every day. Johnson & Johnson has become an essential provider of healthcare and hygiene products, while Procter & Gamble has been at the forefront of innovation in the consumer goods industry.

Finally, we will take a closer look at the sharing economy and the companies that have changed the way we travel and get around. Uber and Lyft have made it easier to get a ride from anywhere in the world, while also creating new opportunities for drivers to earn a living.

Through detailed research and analysis, "New Age Necessities" provides an insightful look into how these companies have become a part of our daily lives, and how they will continue to shape the future of the world. We hope this book will be an eye-opening and informative read for anyone who is interested in the changing landscape of business and technology, and the impact it has on our lives.

Table of Contents

Introduction 10
Shorts.. 14
Chapter: Google 18
Chapter: Amazon 29
Chapter: Apple Inc......................... 37
Chapter: Facebook........................ 45
Chapter: Microsoft......................... 52
Chapter: Coca-Cola....................... 60
Chapter: Visa & Mastercard 69
Chapter: Johnson & Johnson 78
Chapter: Procter & Gamble 86
Chapter: Uber & Lyft 93
Message... 106
Get the Best Out of the Book......... 111
About the Author............................ 114
Summary... 118

Shorts

1. **Google**: The search engine has become the go-to for finding information on just about anything.

2. **Amazon**: The e-commerce giant has revolutionized shopping and become a key player in cloud computing and logistics.

3. **Apple**: The company's iPhones, iPads, and Macs have become ubiquitous in modern life.

4. **Facebook**: The social media platform has connected billions of people around the world.

5. **Microsoft**: Its Windows operating system and Office suite of products are used by millions of people and businesses.

6. **Coca-Cola:** The soft drink giant has a global brand that has become synonymous with refreshment.

7. **Visa and Mastercard**: These two payment processing companies enable the vast majority of online and offline transactions around the world.

8. **Johnson & Johnson**: The company's products range from baby shampoo to medical devices, making it an essential part of many people's lives.

9. **Procter & Gamble**: The company's wide range of household and personal care products, from Tide laundry detergent to Gillette razors, are used by millions of people around the world.

10. **Uber and Lyft**: These ride-hailing services have become essential to many people's daily commutes and transportation needs.

Chapter: Google

Google is a household name that has become synonymous with search engines. Founded in 1998, the company has grown to become a tech giant with a market capitalization of over $1 trillion. Google has become an integral part of modern life, with billions of people around the world using its products and services every day. In this article, we will explore why Google is so important to human life and has become a necessity.

Google Search

Google's primary product is its search engine. Google Search is the most widely used search engine in the world, with over 90% market share. Google Search has become the go-to tool for finding information on just about anything. Whether you're looking for a recipe, researching a topic for school, or trying to find a local business, Google Search can help.

Google's search algorithm is one of the company's most important assets. The algorithm uses hundreds of ranking factors to determine the relevance and quality of web pages. This means that when you search for something on Google, the results are likely to be accurate and helpful.

Google's search engine has become so important to human life that it's difficult to imagine a world without it. People use Google Search to answer questions, solve problems, and make informed decisions. For example, a person might use Google Search to find a doctor or lawyer, research a political candidate, or look up the definition of a word.

Google Maps

Google Maps is another product that has become essential to human life. The mapping and navigation service was launched in 2005 and has since become the go-to tool for finding directions and exploring the world.

Google Maps has revolutionized the way we navigate our daily lives. Whether you're driving to a new city, looking for a restaurant, or trying to find your way around an unfamiliar campus, Google Maps can help. The app provides turn-by-turn directions, real-time traffic updates, and information on nearby businesses and attractions.

Google Maps has also become an important tool for businesses. Companies can use Google Maps to list their location, hours, and contact information, making it easier for customers to find them. For small businesses, Google Maps can be a crucial marketing tool, helping them reach new customers and compete with larger companies.

Google Drive

Google Drive is a cloud storage and collaboration service that allows users to store, share, and edit files online. The service was launched in 2012 and has since become an important tool for individuals and businesses.

Google Drive has several advantages over traditional file storage methods. For one, files stored on Google Drive can be accessed from any device with an internet connection. This means that users can work on the same document from multiple devices, making collaboration much easier.

Google Drive also makes it easy to share files with others. Users can give others permission to view, edit, or comment on their files, making it easy to collaborate on projects. This is particularly useful for businesses, as it allows teams to work together on projects no matter where they are in the world.

Google's Impact on Education

Google's products and services have had a significant impact on education. Google Search has become an essential tool for students and teachers, providing access to a wealth of information on just about any topic. Google Drive has also become an important tool for collaboration and file sharing, making it easier for students to work together on projects.

Google Classroom is another product that has become widely used in education. The platform is a learning management system that allows teachers to create and manage classes, assignments, and grades. Students can access the platform from any device with an internet connection, making it easy to stay organized and up-to-date on their coursework.

Google's impact on education extends beyond its products and services. The company has also invested heavily in education initiatives, such as the Google for Education program. The program provides schools with tools and resources to integrate technology into the classroom, including Chromebooks and free access to G Suite for Education.

Google's impact on education has been significant, allowing for greater access to information, collaboration, and new learning experiences. The company's investments in education have also helped to bridge the digital divide, ensuring that students from all backgrounds have access to technology and the resources they need to succeed.

Google's Impact on Business

Google has had a profound impact on businesses of all sizes. Google Search and Google Maps have made it easier for customers to find businesses and for businesses to reach new customers. Google Ads allows businesses to advertise their products and services to a targeted audience, while Google Analytics provides valuable insights into website traffic and customer behavior.

Google also offers a suite of tools for businesses, including G Suite and Google Cloud Platform. G Suite provides businesses with access to cloud-based tools for email, calendar, document creation, and collaboration. Google Cloud Platform offers a range of cloud-based computing services, including storage, computing, and analytics.

Google's impact on business has been significant, helping companies to reach new customers, streamline their operations, and gain valuable insights into customer behavior. The company's investment in cloud computing has also helped to accelerate digital transformation and innovation, allowing businesses to take advantage of the latest technologies to stay competitive in an increasingly digital world.

The Importance of Google's Culture

Google's success can be attributed in large part to its unique culture. The company has a reputation for innovation, creativity, and a commitment to excellence. Google's culture is built around the concept of "20% time," where employees are encouraged to spend 20% of their workweek pursuing projects that interest them.

This culture of innovation has led to some of Google's most successful products, including Gmail and Google News. The company's commitment to excellence is evident in its focus on user experience and design, which has helped to make Google's products and services easy to use and visually appealing.

Google's culture has also been credited with attracting and retaining top talent. The company offers a range of perks and benefits, including free meals, on-site health care, and generous vacation time. This has helped to create a positive work environment that fosters creativity and innovation.

The Future of Google

As Google continues to innovate and expand its product offerings, its impact on human life is likely to continue to grow. The company has already made significant investments in areas such as artificial intelligence, virtual reality, and self-driving cars, which could have far-reaching implications for society.

Google's commitment to sustainability is also likely to become increasingly important. The company has made a pledge to be carbon neutral by 2020 and has invested heavily in renewable energy. Google's data centers are also among the most efficient in the world, using advanced cooling systems and renewable energy sources to reduce energy consumption.

Conclusion

Google has become an essential part of modern life, providing tools and resources that are essential to daily living, education, and business. The company's search engine, mapping and navigation services, and cloud storage and collaboration tools have revolutionized the way we live and work.

Google's impact on society extends beyond its products and services, with the company's culture of innovation and commitment to sustainability setting an example for others to follow. As Google continues to innovate and expand its product offerings, its impact on human life is likely to continue to grow, shaping the way we live, work, and interact with the world around us.

Chapter: Amazon

Amazon has become a household name in recent years, revolutionizing the way we shop, read, and consume entertainment. From its humble beginnings as an online bookseller, Amazon has evolved into a global e-commerce giant, offering everything from groceries to electronics, and providing a range of digital services such as video streaming and cloud storage. In this article, we will explore the reasons why Amazon has become so important to human life, and why it has become a necessity in the modern world.

The Convenience of Amazon

Perhaps the most obvious reason why Amazon has become so important to human life is its unparalleled convenience. With just a few clicks, consumers can order virtually anything they need, from the comfort of their own homes. Amazon's Prime membership program, which offers free two-day shipping and other benefits, has further enhanced this convenience, allowing consumers to receive their orders faster than ever before.

The convenience of Amazon has changed the way we shop, making it easier and more accessible than ever before. It has also had a profound impact on traditional brick-and-mortar retailers, leading to the closure of many physical stores as consumers increasingly turn to online shopping.

The Range of Products and Services

Another reason why Amazon has become so important to human life is the sheer range of products and services it offers. From books to electronics, groceries to home appliances, Amazon has something for everyone. The company's acquisition of Whole Foods Market has also expanded its offerings to include fresh food and other perishable goods, further increasing its appeal to consumers.

In addition to its vast array of physical products, Amazon has also become a major player in the digital realm. Its video streaming service, Amazon Prime Video, competes with established players such as Netflix and Hulu, while its music streaming service, Amazon Music, competes with Spotify and Apple Music. The company's cloud storage and computing platform, Amazon Web Services (AWS), has also become a key player in the technology industry, providing infrastructure and services to a wide range of businesses and organizations.

The Affordable Prices

Amazon's commitment to offering low prices has also played a significant role in its success. The company's ability to offer products at a lower price than traditional retailers have made it a popular choice for budget-conscious consumers. Its focus on efficiency and automation has helped to reduce costs, enabling the company to pass those savings on to its customers.

The affordable prices offered by Amazon have had a profound impact on human life, allowing consumers to stretch their budgets further and access products and services they might not have been able to afford otherwise. It has also forced other retailers to lower their prices in order to remain competitive.

The Impact on Employment

While Amazon's impact on human life has been largely positive, there are some concerns about the impact the company has had on employment. Critics argue that Amazon's focus on efficiency and automation has led to the displacement of traditional retail jobs, and that its warehouse workers are subject to poor working conditions and low wages.

Amazon has responded to these concerns by investing in robotics and other technologies to improve efficiency and reduce the need for human workers. The company has also committed to paying its employees a minimum wage of $15 per hour and has introduced a range of benefits and programs to support its workers.

Despite these efforts, Amazon's impact on employment is likely to remain a controversial issue, as the company's rapid growth and expansion continue to have a significant impact on the labor market.

The Future of Amazon

As Amazon continues to grow and expand, its impact on human life is likely to continue to grow as well. The company's investments in new technologies, such as artificial intelligence and drone delivery, could have far-reaching implications for the retail industry and the way we consume goods and services.

Amazon's commitment to sustainability is also likely to become increasingly important, as the company seeks to reduce its carbon footprint and address the growing concerns about climate change. The company has already made significant progress in this area, with initiatives such as its Climate Pledge, which commits Amazon to reach net-zero carbon emissions by 2040.

As Amazon continues to innovate and expand its offerings, it is likely to remain a key player in the e-commerce and technology industries for years to come. Its commitment to customer convenience, affordability, and innovation has made it a necessity in the lives of millions of people around the world.

Conclusion

In conclusion, Amazon has become a necessity in human life for several reasons. Its unparalleled convenience, a vast range of products and services, affordable prices, and commitment to innovation have transformed the way we shop and consume goods and services.

While concerns about its impact on employment and the environment remain, it is clear that Amazon has had a profound impact on human life, and is likely to continue to do so in the years to come.

Chapter: Apple Inc.

Apple is one of the most iconic and recognizable brands in the world, known for its sleek and innovative products, such as the iPhone, iPad, and Macbook. In this article, we will explore the reasons why Apple has become so important to human life, and why it has become a necessity in the modern world.

The Design and User Experience

Perhaps the most obvious reason why Apple has become so important to human life is its commitment to design and user experience. Apple products are known for their elegant design, intuitive interfaces, and seamless integration across devices. The company's design philosophy is centered around simplicity, elegance, and functionality, and has been a key factor in its success.

Apple's commitment to design and user experience has had a profound impact on the way we interact with technology, setting a new standard for ease of use and aesthetic appeal. It has also inspired other companies to prioritize design and user experience in their products, leading to an overall improvement in the quality of technology products.

The Ecosystem

Another reason why Apple has become so important to human life is its ecosystem of products and services. Apple offers a range of products, from iPhones to iPads to Macbooks, that seamlessly integrate with each other, creating a unified and connected experience for users. The company's software and services, such as iCloud, Apple Music, and the App Store, further enhance this ecosystem, providing a seamless and integrated experience across devices.

The Apple ecosystem has become a necessity for many users, who rely on it for their daily tasks and entertainment. It has also had a profound impact on the technology industry, inspiring other companies to create their own ecosystems and prioritize integration and connectivity across devices.

The Innovation

Apple's commitment to innovation is another reason why it has become so important to human life. The company has a history of pioneering new technologies, from the graphical user interface to the touchscreen smartphone. Its focus on innovation has resulted in a range of groundbreaking products, such as the iPhone and the Apple Watch, that have changed the way we communicate, access information, and consume entertainment.

Apple's commitment to innovation has also had a broader impact on the technology industry, inspiring other companies to push the boundaries of what is possible with technology. It has also resulted in the creation of new industries, such as the app economy, which has become a significant contributor to the global economy.

The Privacy and Security

Privacy and security have become increasingly important issues in the modern world, and Apple has been at the forefront of addressing these concerns. The company's commitment to privacy and security has been a key factor in its success and has helped to differentiate it from other technology companies.

Apple's products and services are designed with privacy and security in mind, and the company has implemented a range of measures to protect user data and information. Its commitment to privacy and security has earned the trust of millions of users, who rely on Apple products for their security and privacy needs.

The Impact on Education and Creativity

Apple's commitment to education and creativity is another reason why it has become so important to human life. The company has a long history of supporting education, providing students and educators with access to affordable and innovative technology products. Its products, such as the iPad and Macbook, have become essential tools for students and educators around the world, helping to transform the way we learn and teach.

Apple has also had a profound impact on the creative industries, providing artists, musicians, and filmmakers with the tools they need to create and produce their work. Its products, such as Final Cut Pro and Logic Pro, have become essential tools for creative professionals, helping to shape the way we consume and produce entertainment.

As technology continues to advance, Apple's commitment to design, innovation, and privacy and security will likely become even more important. The company has already begun to explore new technologies, such as augmented reality and artificial intelligence, which have the potential to transform the way we interact with technology even further.

However, Apple's success has not been without its controversies. The company has faced criticism for its pricing, labor practices, and closed ecosystem. Some have argued that Apple's products are too expensive, making them inaccessible to many people around the world. Others have criticized the company's labor practices, particularly in its overseas factories, where workers have faced long hours, low wages, and poor working conditions. Additionally, some have argued that Apple's closed ecosystem is limiting, as it restricts users from accessing certain apps and services.

Conclusion

In conclusion, Apple has become a necessity in human life for several reasons. Its commitment to design and user experience, an ecosystem of products and services, innovation, privacy and security, and impact on education and creativity have transformed the way we interact with technology and have had a profound impact on the world. Apple's products have become essential tools for millions of people around the world, helping them to communicate, learn, create, and consume entertainment.

Chapter: Facebook

Facebook is one of the most popular social media platforms in the world, with over 2.9 billion monthly active users as of 2021. In this article, we will explore the reasons why Facebook has become so important to human life and why it has become a necessity in the modern world.

Connectivity

One of the main reasons why Facebook has become so important to human life is its ability to connect people from all over the world. Facebook allows users to create a profile, connect with friends and family, join groups, and follow pages. This has made it easier for people to stay connected with their loved ones, regardless of their location.

Facebook has also become a valuable tool for businesses, organizations, and public figures to connect with their audiences. The platform allows them to create pages, share updates and news, and interact with their followers, increasing their reach and engagement.

Facebook's connectivity has had a profound impact on the way we communicate and interact with each other. It has helped to break down barriers and bring people from different cultures and backgrounds together.

Information Sharing

Another reason why Facebook has become so important to human life is its ability to share information quickly and easily. Users can share updates, photos, videos, and links with their friends and followers, allowing them to keep up to date with the latest news and events.

Facebook's news feed has become a valuable source of information for many people, providing them with access to a wide range of news and perspectives. This has made it easier for people to stay informed about current events, social issues, and other important topics.

Facebook's information-sharing capabilities have also had a profound impact on the media industry, providing publishers and journalists with a new way to reach audiences and share their content.

Community Building

Facebook's group feature has become a valuable tool for community building, allowing users to connect with others who share similar interests and passions. Groups can be created for a wide range of topics, from local community groups to global interest groups.

Facebook's group feature has helped to create new communities and strengthen existing ones, providing a space for people to share their experiences, knowledge, and ideas. This has had a profound impact on the way we connect and interact with each other, providing opportunities for people to find support, friendship, and belonging.

Marketing and Advertising

Facebook has become a powerful tool for businesses and marketers, providing them with access to a large and engaged audience. The platform allows businesses to create pages, advertise their products and services, and interact with their customers, increasing their reach and engagement.

Facebook's advertising capabilities have had a profound impact on the advertising industry, providing businesses with a new way to reach audiences and promote their products and services. The platform's targeting capabilities allow businesses to reach specific demographics and interests, increasing the effectiveness of their advertising campaigns.

Privacy Concerns

Despite its many benefits, Facebook has also faced criticism for its handling of user data and privacy concerns. The platform has been accused of allowing third-party apps to access user data without their consent and failing to adequately protect user data from misuse and abuse.

Facebook's privacy concerns have raised important questions about the role of social media in our lives and the responsibility of technology companies to protect user data. The company has taken steps to address these concerns, such as implementing new privacy policies and increasing its focus on user data protection.

Conclusion

In conclusion, Facebook has become a necessity in human life for several reasons. Its connectivity, information-sharing capabilities, community building, and marketing and advertising capabilities have transformed the way we communicate, connect, and do business. However, Facebook's privacy concerns have raised important questions about the role of social media in our lives and the responsibility of technology companies to protect user data.

Chapter: Microsoft

Microsoft is a multinational technology company that is best known for its software products such as Windows, Microsoft Office, and Microsoft Teams. In this article, we will explore the reasons why Microsoft has become so important to human life and why it has become a necessity in the modern world.

Background

Microsoft was founded by Bill Gates and Paul Allen in 1975. The company started as a small software development company but quickly grew into a major player in the technology industry. Over the years, Microsoft has become known for its operating systems, productivity software, and gaming consoles.

Windows Operating System

One of the main reasons why Microsoft has become so important to human life is its Windows operating system. Windows is the most widely used operating system in the world, with over 1.3 billion users. It has become a vital part of our daily lives, used in everything from personal computers to servers to smartphones.

Windows has had a profound impact on the way we work, communicate, and access information. It has made it easier for people to create, share, and access information, increasing productivity and efficiency. Windows has also made it easier for businesses to manage their operations and access information, improving their decision-making capabilities.

Microsoft Office

Another reason why Microsoft has become so important to human life is its productivity software, Microsoft Office.

Microsoft Office includes programs such as Word, Excel, PowerPoint, and Outlook, which have become essential tools for many people in their daily lives.

Microsoft Office has had a profound impact on the way we work and communicate. It has made it easier for people to create and share documents, presentations, and spreadsheets, improving collaboration and productivity. Microsoft Office has also become an important tool for businesses, providing them with the tools they need to manage their operations and communicate with their customers.

Cloud Computing

In recent years, Microsoft has become a major player in the cloud computing industry. Microsoft Azure is a cloud computing platform that provides a wide range of services, including computing, storage, and networking. Azure has become a valuable tool for businesses, providing them with the ability to store and process large amounts of data, access computing power on demand, and scale their operations quickly and easily.

Microsoft's cloud computing capabilities have had a profound impact on the way we do business. Cloud computing has made it easier for businesses to manage their operations, access information, and communicate with their customers. It has also made it easier for individuals to store and access their data, improving their ability to work and communicate from anywhere in the world.

Gaming

Microsoft's gaming division, Xbox, has become an important part of the company's portfolio. Xbox has become one of the most popular gaming consoles in the world, with over 50 million users.

Xbox has had a profound impact on the gaming industry, providing gamers with a platform to connect and compete with each other. It has also become an important tool for entertainment, providing users with access to streaming services such as Netflix and Hulu.

Artificial Intelligence

Microsoft has also become a major player in the artificial intelligence industry. Microsoft's AI capabilities include services such as Microsoft Cognitive Services, which provides developers with tools to create intelligent applications, and Microsoft Bot Framework, which allows developers to create intelligent chatbots.

Microsoft's AI capabilities have had a profound impact on the way we do business and communicate. AI has made it easier for businesses to automate processes, improve customer service, and access insights from data. AI has also made it easier for individuals to communicate with technology, improving their ability to access information and services.

Conclusion

In conclusion, Microsoft has become a necessity in human life for several reasons. Its Windows operating system, productivity software, cloud computing capabilities, gaming division, and AI capabilities have transformed the way we work, communicate, and access information. Microsoft's impact on the technology industry has been profound, and its innovations have had a significant impact on human life. As technology continues to evolve, it is likely that Microsoft will continue to play a vital role in shaping the future.

Microsoft's products and services have become an integral part of our daily lives, and it is difficult to imagine a world without them. Windows has become the backbone of modern computing, and Microsoft Office has become an essential tool for productivity. Azure has become a valuable tool for businesses, providing them with the ability to store and process large amounts of data. Xbox has become an important part of the gaming industry, and Microsoft's AI capabilities are transforming the way we do business and communicate.

Microsoft has also been a leader in promoting innovation and supporting startups. The company has invested in several startups, providing them with the funding and resources they need to bring their ideas to life. Microsoft has also launched several initiatives aimed at promoting innovation, including the Microsoft Innovation Center and the Microsoft Garage.

Microsoft has also been committed to corporate social responsibility. The company has launched several initiatives aimed at promoting digital inclusion, providing technology access to underserved communities, and supporting education.

Chapter: Coca-Cola

Coca-Cola is one of the most recognized brands in the world. The company has been around for over 130 years and has become an integral part of modern society. Coca-Cola has been a staple of American culture for decades, and its reach has now extended to all corners of the globe. Despite its popularity, some people may wonder why Coca-Cola is so important to human life and has become a necessity. In this article, we will explore the history of Coca-Cola, its impact on society, and the reasons why it has become such an essential part of human life.

History of Coca-Cola

Coca-Cola was invented in 1886 by a pharmacist named John Pemberton. Pemberton was looking for a cure for headaches and invented a concoction made from coca leaves and kola nuts. The original formula contained small amounts of cocaine, which Pemberton believed had medicinal properties. Coca-Cola was initially sold as a tonic and was marketed as a cure-all for a variety of ailments.

Over the years, the formula for Coca-Cola has undergone several changes. The most significant change occurred in 1903 when the company removed cocaine from the formula. Coca-Cola still contains caffeine, which is a stimulant, but it no longer contains any illegal drugs.

Impact on Society

Coca-Cola has had a significant impact on society. The company's marketing campaigns have become iconic, and its influence on popular culture cannot be overstated. Coca-Cola has been associated with everything from Christmas to the Olympics, and its iconic red and white branding is recognized all over the world.

Coca-Cola has also had a significant impact on the economy. The company is one of the largest employers in the United States, and it has a presence in over 200 countries. Coca-Cola's bottling plants and distribution centers employ thousands of people, and the company's suppliers also benefit from its massive demand for sugar, aluminum, and other raw materials.

In addition to its economic impact, Coca-Cola has also had a significant impact on public health. The company has been criticized for its role in the obesity epidemic, and its sugary drinks have been linked to a variety of health problems. Coca-Cola has responded to these criticisms by launching initiatives aimed at promoting healthy lifestyles and reducing its sugar content.

Reasons for Coca-Cola's Popularity

There are several reasons why Coca-Cola has become such an essential part of human life. One of the main reasons is the company's marketing. Coca-Cola's advertising campaigns have been some of the most successful in history, and its branding is recognized all over the world. The company has also been successful in creating an emotional connection with its customers, and its products are often associated with happy memories and special occasions.

Another reason for Coca-Cola's popularity is its accessibility. Coca-Cola is available in almost every corner of the world, and its products are sold in a variety of formats, including cans, bottles, and fountain drinks. The company has also been successful in adapting its products to local tastes, and its products are available in a variety of flavors to cater to different markets.

Coca-Cola's success can also be attributed to its product quality. The company has strict quality control standards, and its products are made with high-quality ingredients. Coca-Cola's manufacturing processes are also highly efficient, which allows the company to produce large quantities of its products at a low cost.

Finally, Coca-Cola's success can be attributed to its ability to innovate. The company has launched several new products over the years, including Diet Coke, Coca-Cola Zero, and Sprite. Coca-Cola has also been at the forefront of packaging innovation, and its products are now available in a variety of eco-friendly formats.

Corporate Social Responsibility

Coca-Cola has been committed to corporate social responsibility since its inception. The company has launched several initiatives aimed at promoting sustainability, reducing its carbon footprint, and supporting local communities.

One of Coca-Cola's most significant sustainability initiatives is its water stewardship program. The company has committed to replenishing 100% of the water it uses in its products and production processes by 2030. Coca-Cola has also launched several initiatives aimed at reducing its carbon footprint, including investing in renewable energy and improving its manufacturing processes to reduce energy consumption.

Coca-Cola is also committed to supporting local communities. The company has launched several initiatives aimed at improving access to clean water, supporting education, and promoting healthy lifestyles. Coca-Cola has also been involved in disaster relief efforts, providing support to communities affected by natural disasters and other crises.

Controversies

Despite its commitment to corporate social responsibility, Coca-Cola has faced several controversies over the years. One of the most significant controversies was its role in the obesity epidemic. Coca-Cola's sugary drinks have been linked to a variety of health problems, including obesity, type 2 diabetes, and heart disease.

Coca-Cola has also been criticized for its environmental impact. The company's plastic bottles and packaging have been linked to pollution and the degradation of natural habitats. Coca-Cola has responded to these criticisms by launching several initiatives aimed at reducing its environmental impact, including investing in recycling infrastructure and promoting eco-friendly packaging.

Conclusion

Coca-Cola has become an essential part of human life, with its iconic branding, accessibility, product quality, and ability to innovate. The company has had a significant impact on society and the economy, and its marketing campaigns have become iconic. Coca-Cola's commitment to corporate social responsibility is also noteworthy, with the company launching several initiatives aimed at promoting sustainability, supporting local communities, and reducing its environmental impact.

While Coca-Cola has faced several controversies over the years, the company's commitment to improving its social and environmental impact is a positive step forward. Coca-Cola remains a staple of modern society, and its continued success is a testament to its ability to adapt to changing consumer preferences and market conditions.

Chapter: Visa & Mastercard

Visa and Mastercard are two of the most recognized payment networks in the world, with their payment systems being used by millions of people every day. These payment networks have become a necessity in modern life, as people rely on them for their everyday transactions, from paying bills to purchasing goods and services online. This article will explore the history, growth, and importance of Visa and Mastercard, as well as their impact on society.

History

Visa and Mastercard have been around for decades, with both payment networks evolving over time to become the giants they are today. Visa was founded in 1958 by Bank of America as BankAmericard, which was the first consumer credit card program to be offered to the public. In 1976, BankAmericard became Visa and went global, with the network expanding to include banks and financial institutions from around the world.

Mastercard was founded in 1966 as Interbank Card Association (ICA), and its first credit card, the Master Charge, was launched in 1969. In 1979, ICA changed its name to Mastercard, and the network has since expanded to include more than 25,000 financial institutions worldwide.

Growth

Visa and Mastercard have grown significantly over the years, with both payment networks expanding their reach globally. Visa is the largest payment network in the world, with over 3 billion cards in circulation and acceptance at over 44 million merchant locations worldwide. Mastercard, on the other hand, has over 2 billion cards in circulation and acceptance at over 37 million merchant locations worldwide.

Visa and Mastercard have also expanded their services beyond traditional credit and debit card transactions. Both payment networks now offer mobile payment solutions, such as Visa Checkout and Masterpass, which allow users to make payments from their mobile devices. These mobile payment solutions have become increasingly popular in recent years, as more people use their smartphones for everyday transactions.

Importance to Human Life

Visa and Mastercard have become essential to human life, with their payment networks providing a fast, secure, and convenient way to make transactions. People rely on these payment networks for their everyday transactions, such as paying bills, purchasing goods and services online, and withdrawing cash from ATMs. Visa and Mastercard also offer rewards programs and cashback incentives, which incentivize people to use their payment networks for their transactions.

The impact of Visa and Mastercard goes beyond convenience and rewards programs. These payment networks have also played a significant role in the global economy, with their services enabling businesses to accept electronic payments from customers around the world. Visa and Mastercard have also helped to drive financial inclusion, enabling people from all walks of life to participate in the global economy and access financial services.

Security

Visa and Mastercard are renowned for their security features, which ensure that customers' financial information is protected from fraud and theft. Both payment networks use advanced encryption and tokenization technologies to protect customers' data during transactions. Visa and Mastercard also offer fraud detection and prevention tools to their partners, which help to detect and prevent fraudulent transactions.

Social Responsibility

Visa and Mastercard are committed to corporate social responsibility, with both payment networks launching several initiatives aimed at promoting sustainability, supporting local communities, and driving financial inclusion. Visa has launched several initiatives aimed at promoting financial literacy, supporting small businesses, and providing access to financial services in underserved communities. Mastercard has also launched several initiatives aimed at driving financial inclusion, supporting women entrepreneurs, and promoting sustainable business practices.

Controversies

Despite their commitment to corporate social responsibility, Visa and Mastercard have faced several controversies over the years. One of the most significant controversies was their role in facilitating illegal online transactions, such as those related to drugs and other illegal activities. Both payment networks have since tightened their policies to prevent illegal transactions

Another controversy that Visa and Mastercard have faced is related to their fees. The payment networks charge fees to merchants for each transaction, and these fees can be a significant expense for businesses. Some businesses have criticized Visa and Mastercard for their high fees, arguing that they are unfair and contribute to higher prices for consumers.

Additionally, Visa and Mastercard have faced criticism for their role in facilitating transactions related to controversial industries, such as the firearms and tobacco industries. Some people argue that Visa and Mastercard should take a stronger stance on these issues and refuse to process transactions related to controversial industries.

Conclusion

Visa and Mastercard have become essential to human life, with their payment networks providing a fast, secure, and convenient way to make transactions. These payment networks have expanded their services beyond traditional credit and debit card transactions to include mobile payment solutions, which have become increasingly popular in recent years. Visa and Mastercard have also played a significant role in the global economy, driving financial inclusion and enabling businesses to accept electronic payments from customers around the world.

Visa and Mastercard's commitment to corporate social responsibility is commendable, with both payment networks launching several initiatives aimed at promoting sustainability, supporting local communities, and driving financial inclusion. However, they have also faced criticism for their role in facilitating illegal online transactions and their high fees.

Overall, Visa and Mastercard have had a significant impact on society, and their payment networks have become a necessity in modern life. While there is room for improvement, Visa and Mastercard's commitment to innovation, security, and corporate social responsibility make them vital players in the global economy.

Chapter: Johnson & Johnson

Johnson & Johnson is one of the largest healthcare companies in the world, with a history that spans over 130 years. The company's commitment to innovation and social responsibility has made it a trusted name in the healthcare industry. Johnson & Johnson's products have become a necessity in human life, with its healthcare products and medical devices helping people around the world to live healthier and more comfortable lives. In this article, we will explore Johnson & Johnson's history, its role in the healthcare industry, and its impact on human life.

History

Johnson & Johnson was founded in 1886 by Robert Wood Johnson, James Wood Johnson, and Edward Mead Johnson. The company was initially focused on producing sterile surgical dressings and wound care products, which were in high demand at the time due to the high number of injuries and infections resulting from the Civil War. Over time, the company expanded its product line to include dental and pharmaceutical products, as well as baby care and personal hygiene products.

Today, Johnson & Johnson is a multinational corporation with operations in over 60 countries. The company's products are divided into three main business segments: pharmaceuticals, medical devices, and consumer health. The company's pharmaceutical products include treatments for a wide range of medical conditions, such as cancer, HIV/AIDS, and cardiovascular disease. The medical devices segment includes products such as surgical instruments, joint replacements, and diagnostic equipment. The consumer health segment includes well-known brands such as Johnson's Baby, Band-Aid, and Tylenol.

Role in the Healthcare Industry

Johnson & Johnson's products play a crucial role in the healthcare industry. The company's pharmaceutical products are used to treat a wide range of medical conditions, from common ailments such as allergies and headaches to life-threatening diseases such as cancer and HIV/AIDS. Many of Johnson & Johnson's pharmaceutical products have become household names, such as Tylenol, Motrin, and Imodium.

In addition to pharmaceuticals, Johnson & Johnson's medical devices are also critical to the healthcare industry. The company's surgical instruments are used by doctors and nurses around the world to perform surgeries, while its joint replacements help patients to regain mobility and improve their quality of life. Johnson & Johnson's diagnostic equipment also plays an important role in the early detection and treatment of medical conditions.

Finally, Johnson & Johnson's consumer health products are also essential to human life. The company's baby care products, such as Johnson's Baby shampoo and lotion, are trusted by parents around the world to keep their babies clean and healthy. Band-Aid is another well-known brand that is used by millions of people to treat cuts and scrapes, while Tylenol is a go-to pain reliever for people suffering from headaches and other types of pain.

Impact on Human Life

Johnson & Johnson's products have had a significant impact on human life. The company's pharmaceutical products have saved countless lives, from antibiotics that cure infections to cancer treatments that help patients to survive and thrive. Johnson & Johnson's medical devices have also played a critical role in improving the quality of life for patients. Joint replacements, for example, enable people to regain mobility and independence, while diagnostic equipment helps doctors to detect medical conditions early when they are most treatable.

In addition to its healthcare products, Johnson & Johnson's commitment to corporate social responsibility has also had a positive impact on human life. The company's Healthy Future 2015 initiative, for example, aimed to improve the health of people around the world by focusing on five key areas: maternal and child health, HIV/AIDS, tuberculosis, mental health, and non-communicable diseases. The initiative included partnerships with organizations such as UNICEF, the World Health Organization, and the Clinton Global Initiative, and resulted in significant progress in these areas.

Johnson & Johnson has also been a leader in promoting sustainability and environmental responsibility. The company's Healthy Planet 2015 initiative aimed to reduce its environmental impact by focusing on three areas: energy and climate, water and wastewater, and waste reduction and recycling. The company has also made a commitment to using sustainable materials in its products, and to reducing the amount of waste it generates.

Furthermore, Johnson & Johnson has played a significant role in responding to global health crises, such as the COVID-19 pandemic. The company's subsidiary, Janssen Pharmaceuticals, developed a COVID-19 vaccine that has been approved for emergency use by regulatory agencies around the world. Johnson & Johnson has also been involved in efforts to increase access to healthcare in underserved communities, through partnerships with organizations such as the Bill and Melinda Gates Foundation and the African Society for Laboratory Medicine.

Conclusion

Johnson & Johnson's products have become a necessity in human life, with its healthcare products and medical devices helping people around the world to live healthier and more comfortable lives. The company's commitment to innovation and social responsibility has made it a trusted name in the healthcare industry. Johnson & Johnson's products have had a significant impact on human life, from saving countless lives with its pharmaceutical products to improving the quality of life for patients with its medical devices. The company's commitment to corporate social responsibility and environmental sustainability also demonstrates its dedication to making a positive impact on the world. Overall, Johnson & Johnson's products and initiatives have become a necessity in human life, and the company's ongoing commitment to innovation and social responsibility will continue to benefit people around the world for years to come.

Chapter: Procter & Gamble

Procter & Gamble (P&G) is a global consumer goods company that produces a wide range of household and personal care products. The company's products are used by millions of people around the world every day, and its brands have become household names. In this article, we will explore the history of P&G and its impact on human life, as well as its commitment to innovation and corporate social responsibility.

History

P&G was founded in 1837 by two men, William Procter and James Gamble, who were brothers-in-law. The two men were immigrants to the United States, and they met in Cincinnati, Ohio, where they both settled. Procter was a candle maker, and Gamble was a soap maker. The two men formed a partnership to create a new product: a high-quality, affordable soap that would be popular with consumers.

The company's first product was called Ivory Soap, which was introduced in 1879.

Ivory Soap was a huge success, and it helped to establish P&G as a major player in the consumer goods industry. Over the years, P&G has expanded its product line to include a wide range of household and personal care products, including Tide laundry detergent, Pampers diapers, and Crest toothpaste.

Impact on Human Life

P&G's products have had a significant impact on human life, particularly in the areas of hygiene and cleanliness. The company's personal care products, such as soap, shampoo, and toothpaste, help people to maintain good hygiene and prevent the spread of disease. P&G's household products, such as laundry detergent and dish soap, help people to keep their homes clean and sanitary.

One of P&G's most iconic products is Pampers diapers, which have been used by millions of parents around the world. Pampers diapers have made it easier for parents to care for their babies and to keep them clean and dry. This has had a significant impact on the lives of parents and babies alike, making it easier for parents to work outside the home and allowing babies to be more comfortable and content.

In addition to its products, P&G has also made significant contributions to society through its corporate social responsibility initiatives. The company has a long history of supporting charitable causes, including disaster relief efforts and programs to improve access to education and healthcare. P&G has also been a leader in sustainability, with initiatives to reduce its environmental footprint and promote sustainable practices throughout its supply chain.

Commitment to Innovation

P&G has a strong commitment to innovation, with a research and development budget of over $2 billion per year. The company has a dedicated team of scientists and engineers who work to develop new products and improve existing ones. P&G's innovation efforts have led to the creation of many groundbreaking products, including the first synthetic laundry detergent, Tide, and the first disposable diaper, Pampers.

In recent years, P&G has been focusing on innovation in the area of sustainability. The company has set ambitious goals to reduce its environmental footprint, including a commitment to zero deforestation in its supply chain by 2020. P&G has also been working to develop sustainable product packaging and to promote sustainable practices among its suppliers and customers.

Corporate Social Responsibility

P&G has a strong commitment to corporate social responsibility, with initiatives focused on environmental sustainability, community development, and diversity and inclusion. The company has set ambitious goals to reduce its environmental footprint, including a commitment to using 100% renewable energy in its operations by 2030. P&G has also been working to promote sustainable practices throughout its supply chain and to reduce the amount of waste it generates.

Procter & Gamble has also made significant efforts towards sustainability and corporate social responsibility. The company has set ambitious goals to reduce its environmental impact, including a commitment to make its products using 100% renewable or recycled materials by 2030. In addition, the company has made efforts to reduce water usage and increase energy efficiency in its operations. P&G has also launched several social impact programs aimed at improving education, health, and hygiene in communities around the world.

One notable example of P&G's social impact efforts is its Children's Safe Drinking Water program. This initiative provides water purification packets to communities without access to clean drinking water, helping to prevent waterborne illnesses and improve overall health. Since its launch in 2004, the program has provided over 18 billion liters of clean drinking water to people in need around the world.

Conclusion

Procter & Gamble is an incredibly important company that has become a necessity in the lives of billions of people around the world. Its wide range of household products and brands have become household names, and its commitment to innovation and sustainability has made it a leader in the consumer goods industry. The company's social impact programs, including its Children's Safe Drinking Water program, demonstrate P&G's commitment to making a positive difference in the world. Overall, P&G's products and initiatives have touched the lives of countless people, making it a vital part of our daily lives.

Chapter: Uber & Lyft

Uber and Lyft are two of the most well-known ride-hailing services in the world. These companies have revolutionized the way people get around, making transportation more accessible and convenient for millions of people. In this article, we will explore the importance of Uber and Lyft to human life and why they have become a necessity.

Background

Uber was founded in 2009, while Lyft was founded in 2012. Both companies are headquartered in San Francisco and operate in cities around the world. The basic premise of both services is to provide passengers with a ride from point A to point B, with drivers using their personal vehicles to transport passengers. Passengers use a mobile app to hail a ride, and the fare is automatically calculated based on the distance and time of the ride.

Importance to Human Life

Accessibility

One of the primary ways in which Uber and Lyft are important to human life is by increasing accessibility to transportation. In many cities around the world, public transportation options are limited, and owning a car can be expensive. Ride-hailing services like Uber and Lyft offer an affordable and convenient alternative to traditional transportation options. With the touch of a button, passengers can request a ride and be on their way within minutes.

Convenience

Uber and Lyft also offer a level of convenience that traditional transportation options cannot match. Passengers can request a ride from anywhere, at any time, and be picked up in a matter of minutes. This is especially important in situations where time is of the essence, such as getting to a job interview or catching a flight. Additionally, ride-hailing services eliminate the need for passengers to navigate unfamiliar streets or find parking, making transportation easier and less stressful.

Safety

Safety is another important aspect of ride-hailing services. Both Uber and Lyft have implemented extensive safety measures to protect passengers and drivers. Drivers are required to undergo background checks and vehicle inspections, and both companies have implemented rating systems that allow passengers to rate their drivers and provide feedback on their experience. Additionally, both Uber and Lyft have implemented safety features in their apps, such as the ability to share ride details with friends and family and the option to contact emergency services directly from the app.

Job Creation

Uber and Lyft have also had a significant impact on job creation. The companies have created millions of jobs around the world, providing opportunities for people to earn income on their own terms. Many drivers work for Uber and Lyft as a side hustle, using the platforms to supplement their income from a full-time job or to earn extra money in their spare time. Additionally, ride-hailing services have provided opportunities for people who may have difficulties finding traditional employment, such as those with disabilities or those who cannot work traditional hours.

Environmental Impact

Another way in which ride-hailing services are important to human life is by reducing the environmental impact of transportation. By reducing the number of cars on the road, Uber and Lyft have the potential to decrease traffic congestion and air pollution. Additionally, both companies have implemented initiatives aimed at reducing their environmental impact, such as Uber's Clean Air Plan, which aims to have 100% of Uber vehicles in certain cities be electric or hybrid by 2025.

Necessity

Given the numerous ways in which ride-hailing services like Uber and Lyft are important to human life, it is not surprising that they have become a necessity for many people. In many cities around the world, ride-hailing services are the only affordable and convenient transportation option available. In addition, ride-hailing services have become an essential part of many people's daily routines, whether it is commuting to work, running errands, or going out with friends.

Moreover, Uber and Lyft have had a significant impact on the environment. According to a study conducted by the Union of Concerned Scientists, ridesharing services like Uber and Lyft are more environmentally friendly than driving a personal vehicle. The study found that ridesharing services produce 69% fewer emissions than the average personal vehicle, and even greater reductions in emissions are possible with the use of electric or hybrid vehicles. This is an important benefit, considering the pressing need to reduce greenhouse gas emissions and combat climate change.

In addition, Uber and Lyft have created new job opportunities and provided an alternative source of income for many people. Drivers for Uber and Lyft can work flexible hours, and some even make it their full-time job. This has been particularly important for people who are unable to work a traditional 9-to-5 job, such as those with disabilities, caregivers, or students.

Furthermore, Uber and Lyft have made transportation more accessible for people who live in areas with limited public transportation options. This includes people living in rural areas, where public transportation is often not available, and those who cannot afford to own a car or do not have a driver's license. By providing a reliable and affordable transportation option, Uber and Lyft have helped to increase mobility and independence for many people.

However, despite these benefits, Uber and Lyft have faced criticism and controversy over the years. One of the most significant issues has been the treatment of drivers. Critics argue that drivers are not fairly compensated for their work and do not receive benefits such as healthcare, retirement, or paid time off. This has led to protests and legal action by drivers seeking better pay and working conditions.

In addition, there have been concerns about the safety of passengers using these services. This includes incidents of assault and harassment by drivers, as well as accidents involving ridesharing vehicles. Uber and Lyft have taken steps to address these concerns, such as implementing background checks for drivers and improving safety features in their apps. However, more needs to be done to ensure the safety of both drivers and passengers.

Uber and Lyft both have a corporate social responsibility (CSR) program that includes a range of initiatives aimed at addressing social, environmental, and economic issues.

Uber's CSR program includes a focus on sustainability, with a goal to reduce the carbon footprint of its operations. In 2018, Uber announced a commitment to electrify its entire fleet of cars by 2040, and to have at least 5 million electric vehicles on its platform by 2025. The company has also launched a program to encourage drivers to switch to electric vehicles by offering incentives such as lower rental rates and higher pay per ride.

In addition, Uber has launched several initiatives aimed at promoting equality and diversity. This includes a partnership with the National Center for Civil and Human Rights to create a civil rights and equality education program for drivers, and a diversity and inclusion training program for employees. The company has also implemented features in its app to help ensure the safety of transgender and non-binary riders.

Lyft's CSR program includes a focus on sustainability, with a goal to achieve 100% carbon neutrality for its operations. The company has launched several initiatives aimed at reducing the carbon footprint of its rides, such as offering incentives for drivers to use electric or hybrid vehicles and purchasing carbon offsets for all of its rides. Lyft has also committed to transitioning to a fully electric fleet of cars by 2030.

Lyft's CSR program also includes initiatives aimed at promoting diversity and inclusion. The company has established a diversity and inclusion council and has implemented unconscious bias training for employees. Lyft has also launched several programs aimed at increasing access to transportation for underserved communities, such as offering discounted rides to people living in food deserts and partnering with non-profit organizations to provide free rides to people in need.

Both Uber and Lyft have also launched initiatives aimed at addressing the issue of food insecurity. Uber has partnered with food banks and non-profit organizations to provide free meals to people in need, while Lyft has partnered with grocery stores to provide discounted rides to and from stores for people living in food deserts.

Overall, both Uber and Lyft have demonstrated a commitment to CSR through a range of initiatives aimed at addressing social, environmental, and economic issues. While there is always room for improvement, their efforts in this area demonstrate a recognition of their role in society and a commitment to using their platform to create positive change.

Conclusion

Uber and Lyft have revolutionized the transportation industry and have become integral parts of modern life. Their platforms have made it easier and more convenient for people to get around, and their impact on the economy has been significant.

Despite their controversies and challenges, both companies have demonstrated a commitment to corporate social responsibility through a range of initiatives aimed at addressing social, environmental, and economic issues. They have launched sustainability initiatives, diversity and inclusion programs, and initiatives aimed at addressing food insecurity, among others.

As with any company, there is always room for improvement in terms of CSR and addressing societal issues. However, Uber and Lyft's efforts in this area demonstrate a recognition of their role in society and a commitment to using their platform to create positive change.

As the world continues to evolve, it will be interesting to see how Uber and Lyft adapt and innovate to meet the changing needs and demands of consumers, while also continuing to prioritize corporate social responsibility.

Message

The companies discussed in this book have become integral parts of our daily lives, serving as necessities that we rely on for communication, transportation, healthcare, and consumer goods. From the moment we wake up until we go to bed, we interact with these companies in some way or another, often without even realizing it.

These companies have revolutionized the way we live and work, bringing convenience, efficiency, and innovation to our lives. They have become so intertwined with our daily routines that we can hardly imagine life without them.

However, with great power comes great responsibility. These companies have a significant impact on society, and it is essential that they recognize their social and ethical responsibilities. From reducing their environmental impact to ensuring fair labor practices and protecting user privacy, these companies must prioritize their corporate social responsibility.

As consumers, we also have a responsibility to hold these companies accountable and to use our purchasing power to support companies that prioritize social responsibility. By doing so, we can create a better world for ourselves and future generations.

In short, the companies discussed in this book have become necessities, but it is up to us to ensure that they are also responsible corporate citizens. We must work together to build a more sustainable, equitable, and just world.

Notes

Notes

Notes

Get the Best Out of the Book

To get the most out of "New Age Necessities," we recommend reading the book cover to cover in order to gain a comprehensive understanding of the companies and industries covered. Each chapter is dedicated to a specific company or industry and provides an in-depth analysis of its history, products or services, and impact on society.

As you read, we encourage you to take notes and reflect on the insights presented in each chapter. Consider how the company or industry has affected your own life, as well as the lives of those around you. You may also want to consider how the company has impacted the world at large, both in terms of positive changes and potential drawbacks.

Additionally, we recommend taking the time to do additional research on the companies or industries that pique your interest. This book serves as a starting point for understanding the influence of these companies, but there is always more to learn and discover.

Finally, we hope that "New Age Necessities" inspires you to think critically about the role of technology and business in our lives and to consider the ways in which these companies can continue to innovate and positively impact society in the future.

113

About the Author

Sahil A Gosalia is the author of "New Age Necessities." He is a writer and researcher with a passion for technology and its impact on society. He has studied business management and technology at the university level and has extensive experience in the tech industry.

In addition to his writing, Gosalia is also an avid traveler and a lover of all things related to food and culture. He believes that travel broadens the mind and provides valuable perspectives on different ways of life. He is dedicated to making a positive impact on the world and believes that technology can be used for good to improve people's lives.

Overall, Sahil A Gosalia is a knowledgeable and passionate writer with a unique perspective on the intersection of technology and society. **"New Age Necessities"** is the culmination of his research and writing on this topic, and it provides valuable insights into the companies that have become essential to human life.

Scan to check more of my work!

Scan to BUY Books, Journals, Notebooks

Scan to BUY Kindle Edition E-Books

Scan to know more about the Author

Summary

"New Age Necessities" is a book that explores the world's most influential and innovative companies that have become essential to our daily lives. It focuses on the corporations that have disrupted industries, changed the game, and shaped modern society as we know it.

From tech giants like Google, Apple, and Microsoft, to e-commerce powerhouses like Amazon, to essential service providers like Visa and Mastercard, to healthcare and consumer goods companies like Johnson & Johnson and Procter & Gamble, the book delves into the stories of how these companies became indispensable to our lives.

The book also explores the corporate social responsibility initiatives of these companies, showcasing how they have taken on societal, environmental, and economic issues to make a positive impact in the world.

Through detailed research and analysis, "New Age Necessities" provides an insightful look into how these companies have become a part of our daily lives, and how they will continue to shape the future of the world. It highlights the importance of these companies, and why they have become so necessary in the new age we live in.

Scan to check more of my work!

Scan to BUY Books, E-Books, Journals, Notebooks

Scan to know more about the Author

www.ingramcontent.com/pod-product-compliance
Lightning Source LLC
Chambersburg PA
CBHW020438220526

45464CB00002B/751